ISBN 978-1-331-60031-2
PIBN 10211179

1 MONTH OF
FREE
READING

at

www.ForgottenBooks.com

By purchasing this book you are eligible for one month membership to ForgottenBooks.com, giving you unlimited access to our entire collection of over 1,000,000 titles via our web site and mobile apps.

To claim your free month visit:

www.forgottenbooks.com/free211179

English
Français
Deutsche
Italiano
Español
Português

www.forgottenbooks.com

Mythology Photography **Fiction**
Fishing Christianity **Art** Cooking
Essays Buddhism Freemasonry
Medicine **Biology** Music **Ancient**
Egypt Evolution Carpentry Physics
Dance Geology **Mathematics** Fitness
Shakespeare **Folklore** Yoga Marketing
Confidence Immortality Biographies
Poetry **Psychology** Witchcraft
Electronics Chemistry History **Law**
Accounting **Philosophy** Anthropology
Alchemy Drama Quantum Mechanics
Atheism Sexual Health **Ancient History**
Entrepreneurship Languages Sport
Paleontology Needlework Islam
Metaphysics Investment Archaeology
Parenting Statistics Criminology
Motivational

P. B. SHELLEY.

(From a crayon copy of Miss Curran's oil portrait
in the Bodleian Library).

BY D.ʳ GUIDO BIAGI. ✤

Librarian of the Laurentian Library, ?

LONDON – T. FISHER UNWIN, MDCCCXCVIII.

BY D.ʳ GUIDO BIAGI. ✤

Librarian of the Laurentian Library, Fl.

LONDON – T. FISHER UNWIN, MDCCCXCVIII.

TO

LADY SHELLEY

THE WORTHY GUARDIAN

OF AN IMMORTAL TRUST

LIST OF ILLUSTRATIONS.

1. P. B. SHELLEY. -- (From a crayon copy of Miss
   Curran's oil portrait in the Bodleian Library)
   . . . . *To face* p.   1
2. P. B. SHELLEY. — (From a copy, by Reginald
   Easton, of the Duke de Montpensier's miniature
   of Shelley, in the Bodleian Library). *To face* p.   8
3. EDWARD ELLERKER WILLIAMS, Painted by
   himself. — (From the water colour original, in
   possession of Mr. J. W. Williams of West
   Norwood) . . . . *To face* p. 15
4. JANE WILLIAMS, Painted by Clint. — (From the
   original portrait, in possession of Mr. J. W.
   Williams). . . . . *To face* p. 17
5. THE GUITAR GIVEN BY SHELLEY TO JANE
   WILLIAMS. — (Bodleian Library). *To face* p. 18
6. MARY WOLLSTONECRAFT. — (From the
   Miniature by Reginald Easton, in the Bodleian
   Library). . . . . *To face* p. 21
7. CASA MAGNI, AT SAN TERENZO . *To face* p. 26
8. CASA MAGNI AND THE WOOD . . *To face* p. 29

9. THE TWO YACHTS " BOLIVAR " AND " DON
   JUAN ". — (From a sketch by E. E. Williams,
   in the British Museum) . . . . *To face* p.   33
10. LEIGH HUNT. — (From the picture by B. R.
    Haydon in the National Portrait Gallery. By
    kind permission of Messrs Walker & Boutall,
    London). . . . . *To face* p.   41
11. MONUMENT TO KEATS AT ROME . *To face* p.   72
12. THE 'SOPHOCLES' TAKEN FROM SHELLEY'S
    DEAD HAND. — (Bodleian Library). *To face* p.   81
13. EDWARD WYNDHAM HARRINGTON SCHENLEY.
    (Born 1800, died 1878). . . . . *To face* p. 107
14. EDGE OF PINE WOOD AT VIAREGGIO. — (From
    Biagi's photograph, reproduced in " *Harper's
    Magazine*", 1892) . . . . . . *To face* p. 120
15. SHELLEY'S WATCH AND CHAIN AND HIS SIGNET
    TOGETHER WITH THAT OF HIS WIFE. — (Bo-
    dleian Library) . . . . *To face* p. 129
16. THE EIGHT WITNESSES OF SHELLEY'S CREMATION.
    — (From Biagi's photograph reproduced in
    " *Harper's Magazine*" 1892) . . *To face* p. 156
17. MONUMENT TO SHELLEY AT VIAREGGIO. . .
    . . . . *To face* p. 160
18. THE TOMBS TO SHELLEY AND TRELAWNY AT
    ROME. . . . . *To face* p. 165
19. SHELLEY'S TOMBSTONE AT ROME . *To face* p. 167

The Last Days of P. B. Shelley

To those whose hearts have thrilled over the pages of Trelawney and the narratives of other witnesses to these facts, as well as those of Professor Dowden's masterly biography of the poet, related, as it is with the true insight of love; it were idle once more to recount the bare details of that dark catastrophe which closed, tragically as an antique drama woven by inevitable Fate, the life of Percy Bysshe Shelley.

Who, in truth, can remember without profound sympathy, I had almost said, without tears, that sorrowful letter which Mary Shelley, the desolate widow, wrote on the 15th of August, 1822, to Mrs. Gisborne telling the story of those days of agony? The terrible drama of which those two women, Mrs. Shelley, and Mrs. Williams foresaw the end, is narrated with so true, so natural a *crescendo* of horror and of pathos as might move even the author of ' The Real Shelley ', if certain critics condescended to possess hearts. If no more were known of Shelley's beloved companion, this letter would be enough to prove how worthy she was to be invoked as "Mine own heart's home", as he calls her in the dedication of the ' Revolt of Islam ', in which he says: " through thine eyes, even in thy soul I see, A Lamp of vestal fire, burning internally ".

" The days pass ", she writes after the terrible event, " pass one after another, and we still live. ' Adonais' is not Keats' elegy, but his very own". Who knows how often she read, and re-read it in those twentynine long years during which she outlived him, widowed vestal of her one and only love ? The proof is found in a copy of the Pisan edition of this poem, that she possessed, where after her death a tiny silken sack was found among the pages, containing ashes, taken by her from his funeral urn.

So is it in all which concerns
the poet of the " Liberated World ",
there breathes the true and simple
grandeur of the *pathos* of the days
of old.

Whoever thinks over this sorrowful story, to which we contribute a few documents hitherto unknown, wonders at the mysterious omens which announce the imminent catastrophe. Over Shelley's life there broods a strange fate, from which he strives in vain to free himself: he is the principal actor in an actual drama which unfolds itself according to an occult plan. He was sadly conscious of it. " It seems " he says " as

if I were consumed by destruction,
as if a fatal atmosphere enfolded and
infected all that belongs to me ".[1]

The death of the unfortunate
Harriet, his first wife, deserted by
him with truly Goethian indifference,
weighed upon his soul; and the
image of the unhappy girl drowned
in the waters of the Serpentine shaded
with a mournful veil the years in
which he sought comfort in the love
and the embraces of Mary, and in
platonic devotion to other ideals.
Water had for him a sort of magic
attraction; he might have made his
own, in a literal sense, a line written by another inconsolable poet,

---

[1] Quoted by Dowden. II. 252.

Leopardi: " And sweet it is to drown in such a sea ".

The idea of such an ending to his life had for him no terrors; one of his favourite hobbies was to set afloat a squadron of paper boats and to follow their movements with his eyes, lost in a sort of ecstasy. " Without doubt ", says Dowden, "while he watched them float from the shore, guided by the wind, those paper toys became for him objects of joy and wonder, like the pearly chariot of Queen Mab, or like the little boat which bore the lonely dreamer far out to sea from the Corasmian shore. It was strange to see with what acute delight he grew absorbed in this singular oc-cupation. As long as the boats were

visible, he remained rooted to the
spot, as if fascinated by this strange
amusement ".[1]

Once while he watched such
paper boats across the pond at the
Vale of Health, floating before the
wind or sinking beneath the waves,
he said smiling: " How happy should
I be if I could get into one of those
boats and be shipwrecked, it must
be the most desirable of all forms of
death ".

With this fixed idea in his head
he was always rushing into danger,
and was often nearly drowned, beholding death close upon him. With
Mary Woolstonecraft Godwin, flying

---

[1] Dowden, I. 477.

P. B. SHELLEY.

(From a copy, by Reginald Easton, of the Duke de Montpensier's miniature of Shelley, in the Bodleian Library).

F. R. SMITH.

across the Channel, when he bore her away from her father's house, he was nearly shipwrecked. The girl lay with her head upon her lover's knees, unwitting of the tempest. " I felt " he says " that she was there. At that moment I had time for reflection and meditation upon death; and I felt more discomfort and disillusion than horror ".

On the lake of Geneva, while visiting with Byron those scenes, so full of memories of Rousseau, they were caught in a "*fortunale* " and their fragile bark was nearly lost through the want of skill of their boatman. - " My companion (Byron), an excellent swimmer, took off his coat; I did the same, and we sat with folded arms expecting every moment to be upset. Seeing death so near, I experienced a mixture of sensations, among which fear held by no means the first place. If I had been alone, my sensations would have been less painful; but I knew that my companion would have tried to rescue me, and I felt humiliated at the thought that his life might be vainly sacrificed to save mine ". [1]

Another time, scarcely a year before the fatal shipwreck, he was sailing between Leghorn and Pisa in a fragile craft, with Captain Williams and Henry Reveley, Mrs. Gisborne's son, who was a sailor and an engi-

[1] Dowden, II, 17.

neer. Williams took it into his head to climb up the mast, and the boat was upset. At that point the water was very deep; Reveley assisted Williams, who could swim a little, and told Shelley not to move until he came back for him. Shelley replied with indomitable courage, " All right, I never was better off in my life, do what you like with me ".

Towards the last, this passion for the water became absolutely morbid. With boats which preoccupied him constantly he had no luck. " I see how it is, " he said, "they are feminine ships and boats, and perfidious like women ".

At San Terenzo he sailed about thoughtlessly in a sort of canoe made of canvass and reeds. One evening he persuaded Jane Williams, with her children, to embark in this fragile craft with him. She thought he meant to keep close to the shore, but Shelley started to round a cape which jutted out into the open sea.

Not a soul was visible either at sea or on shore. The boat went floating out to sea and the poet seemed wrapped in a dream. He would not answer, would not listen to the poor woman, who, half mad with terror, strove to wake him from his lethargy. Suddenly Shelley, raising his head with a radiant aspect, exclaimed " Now let us go together to solve the great mystery ". But Jane, who felt no such curiosity, replied: " No, thank you, not now. I prefer to go back to supper with my children ". And by questions and conversation she brought him back to more mundane thoughts.

Williams and Trelawney, (who was then a guest at Casa Magni), were waiting for them on the shore, in no small anxiety. Jane, as they drew near the beach, leaped out of the boat which fell back with the poet. When Williams remonstrated with her, saying he would have drawn the boat on shore if she had waited a minute, " No thank you, " she cried, still much agitated, " I have had enough of it. He wanted to solve the great mystery. But he is the greatest mystery. Who can tell what he will do next? ".

Once more, the demon of the sea, who was watching for his prey, had spread his wings and flown.

EDWARD ELLERKER WILLIAMS
Painted by himself.

(From the water colour original, in possession ot Mr. J.
W. Williams of West Norwood).

II

On the evening of January 15th 1822, the Shelleys and the Williams' were together in the small apartment which they had taken on the upper floor of a house which went by the name of the *Tre Palazzi di Chiesa* (The Three Palaces of the Chiesa family) situated on the Lung'Arno at Pisa, opposite to the Palazzo Lanfranchi where Lord Byron was residing.

The Shelleys and the Williams' were very intimate and for nearly a year had been living together. Edward Williams, who had been Shelley's schoolfellow at Eton, had come from Geneva into Italy, on purpose to make the acquaintance of Byron of whom Medwin had spoken to him with the warmest enthusiasm. He had served in the navy, but disgusted with the discipline, then of an inexcusably tyrannical character, had entered a dragoon regiment, remaining several years in India. Frank, generous, loyal, intrepid, with a passion for travelling and for the sea, an enthusiast for art, he could not fail to please Shelley.

His wife, Jane Williams, possessed a natural grace of her own, which won everybody whom she met.

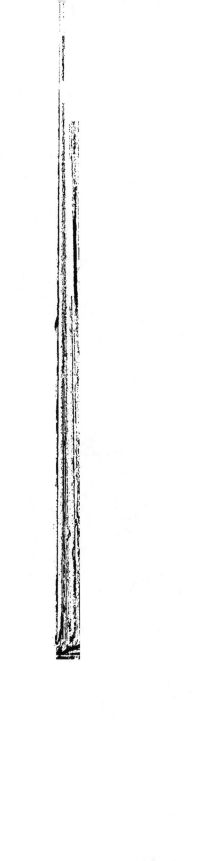

JANE WILLIAMS, Painted by Clint.

(From the original portrait, in possession of Mr. J. W. Williams).

She was one of those sparkling little women whose every act and movement is full of fascination. An accomplished musician, she sang deliciously, with a sweet, full, touching voice, accompanying herself on the harp. She was not highly cultivated, but was full of delicacy aud tact. An atmosphere of happiness and comfort surrounded her. To Shelley, who took to her immediately, Jane, with her' grace, her suavity, the gentleness of her movements and her ways of speaking, seemed the bringer of the most ideal sweetness, in which, after her husband, friends such as he was, were admitted to share. Poems of his, written at that period, idealize her under various names. She is Miran-

da, whose gentleness, charity and
ineffable tenderness are celebrated by
Ariel. She seemed a spirit formed for
peace, in the midst of tempests. With
the gift of a guitar he writes to her:

" Teach it all the harmony
" In which thou canst, and only thou,
" Make the delighted spirit glow,
" Till joy denies itself again
" And, too intense, is turned to pain ".

The little apartment in the *Tre
Palazzi di Chiesa,* with its southern
exposure looking towards the mountains and the sea, which Shelley called his " pensile citadel " where grew
the flowers immortalized in " The
Zucca, " the " Sensitive plant " and
other poems, sheltered, that night, a
new guest, a new friend who had ar-

THE GUITAR GIVEN BY SHELLEY
TO JANE WILLIAMS.

(Bodleian Library).

rived the day before. Edward Trelawney, who had conceived a strong
affection for Shelley (of whom
Medwin had talked to him in Geneva
with his usual fanatical admiration)
had come to Pisa to meet him and to
carry off Williams to hunt that win-
ter in the Maremma, with an old naval comrade, Captain Daniel Roberts.
Trelawney pleased Shelley, as Williams had done in the previous year;
but the new friend was an entirely
different type of man. Very tall, with
black hair, as curly as a moor's,
black expressive eyes and heavy
eyebrows, he looked like an oriental.
His smile, which was open and hon-
est, was a proof of sincerity and of
a superior mind. We find an idealized

portrait of him in the " Fragments of an unfinished Drama ".

" He was as is the sun in his fierce youth
" As terrible and lovely as a tempest ".

Shelley made an ineffaceable impression on him. He was struck with the poet's eyes, of a vast, wonderful brightness, drawn as it were from the pages of Plato, of Spinoza, of Calderon and of Goethe, in the reading of which he loved to lose himself. " Spirito di Titano entro virginee forme " one of our own (Italian) poets has called him " A Titan's spirit in a Virgin's form ". But Trelawney did not look upon Shelley in this light. " I often saw him naked, " he says, " and he reminded

MARY WOLLSTONECRAFT.

(From the Miniature by Reginald Easton, in the Bodleian Library).

me of a young Indian, so muscular and wiry was he. None of us could outwalk him, he was the swiftest of us all. He was brave, frank, simple and direct in speech, courteous and considerate of others, being entirely free from selfishness or vanity.

As for Mary, the poet's gentle companion, who shared his studies, who loved and comforted him, confident and trusting as an indulgent mother, superior to all feminine distrust, it is enough to say that she had never descended from the pedestal on which the first enthusiasm of love had placed her, that from that ideal height she smiled upon the lover, the husband, with the serenity of a Madonna and the tenderness of a mother.

III

On that memorable evening the
project, often before discussed by
Williams and Shelley, of passing the
summer together near Spezia, was
mentioned once more. But a boat
was needed, and Trelawney had been
written to, that he might induce
Captain Roberts to superintend its
construction. Trelawney had brought
with him the model of an American
schooner, and naturally this formed
the subject of their conversation. It
was decided that a sloop thirty feet

long should be built, and Captain Roberts at Genoa was requested to have
it begun at once. " So on that night,
a night of thoughtless amusement, "
writes Mrs. Shelley, poor woman,
later on, " was my unhappy fate and
Jane's decided. We said laughingly:
' Our husbands decide everything
without our advice or consent '. In
fact, for my part, I hated the idea
of the boat, though I said nothing to
them about it. Jane said she also did,
but it would be of no use talking
to them, it would only spoil their
pleasure. How well I remember that
night! How short-sighted we are!
The terrible anniversary is past
already, and I cannot believe in
my own wretchedness ".

Soon after this, they began to look for a villa for the summer. Byron was to form part of the colony, as well as Countess Guiccioli and Pietro Gamba, Trelawney and Captain Roberts. The early days of spring with their bright sunshine, limpid sky and flowering hedges, were well adapted for such excursions. The two friends, Shelley and Williams, explored the gulf of Spezia, to very little purpose.

Meanwhile circumstances occurred which modified the design of this *villeggiatura* in common. The quarrel with Sergeant-Major Masi, in which Shelley ran the risk of losing his life, made it clear to Byron (whose *bravo* Giovanni Battista Folcieri, called Titta, was accused of having seriously wounded the dragoon) that it was wiser to get out of the way. On the other hand the long residence on intimate terms with the other poet had shown Shelley what kind of man Byron was. His conduct to poor Claire Clairmont, who was a connection of the Godwins, and whom he had seduced and then abandoned; the cruelty with which he prevented her from seeing her child, the little Allegra, who was shut up in a poverty-stricken little Capuchin Convent at Bagnacavallo, in which prison she died; the facility with which he gave credit to the calumnies invented by two discharged servants regarding Shelley and Claire, calumnies against which Mary Shelley herself protested with proud sincerity; – (Byron, by the way, found them very convenient when he wished to justify the *clausura* of the child); Shelley was disgusted and repelled by all these unworthy proceedings. Spend the summer with him! Never! All he wished was to get as far away from him as possible.

The search for the wished for summer residence was resumed, but now only for the Williams and the Shelleys. They were at last compelled to content themselves with Casa Magni (now called Villa Maccarani) on the gulf of Spezia. Hither they transported their furniture by sea, and took up their abode on May 1st 1822.

" No more splendid frame " writes Mantegazza " could have been found

CASA MAGNI, AT SAN TERENZO.

for Shelley's genius; no dwelling
more worthy of his transcendental
idealism, of his.

'High spirit-winged heart'.

It is a rugged old house, standing
as it were, with its feet in the sea,
with a mountain behind it covered
with evergreen ilex and pine trees.
Solitary it is, and strong as a fortress,
with a terrace and porch opening on
the sea. More like a ship than a
house, the sea enters the porch as if
by right, bathes the walls and often
sends a salt greeting even to the
inhabitants of the first floor and the
terrace. These savage embraces have
given to the house still called " Shelley's Villa " the rugged and wrinkled

aspect of some ancient mariner. The iron railings are eaten away like old cheese with rust, and on the weather beaten bricks the sea salt sparkles and the nitre creeps in wavy lines ". The poet raved of it: " I still dwell in this divine bay ", he writes " reading Spanish plays and listening to the divinest music ". This was an allusion to Jane Williams' singing, as she accompanied herself on the guitar that Ariel had given to Miranda.

But Mary, who was expecting her confinement, and far from well, could not bear the place; its glowing beauty jarred on her strained and delicate nerves. The house seemed to her desolate, and a " presentiment of coming misfortune weighed upon her

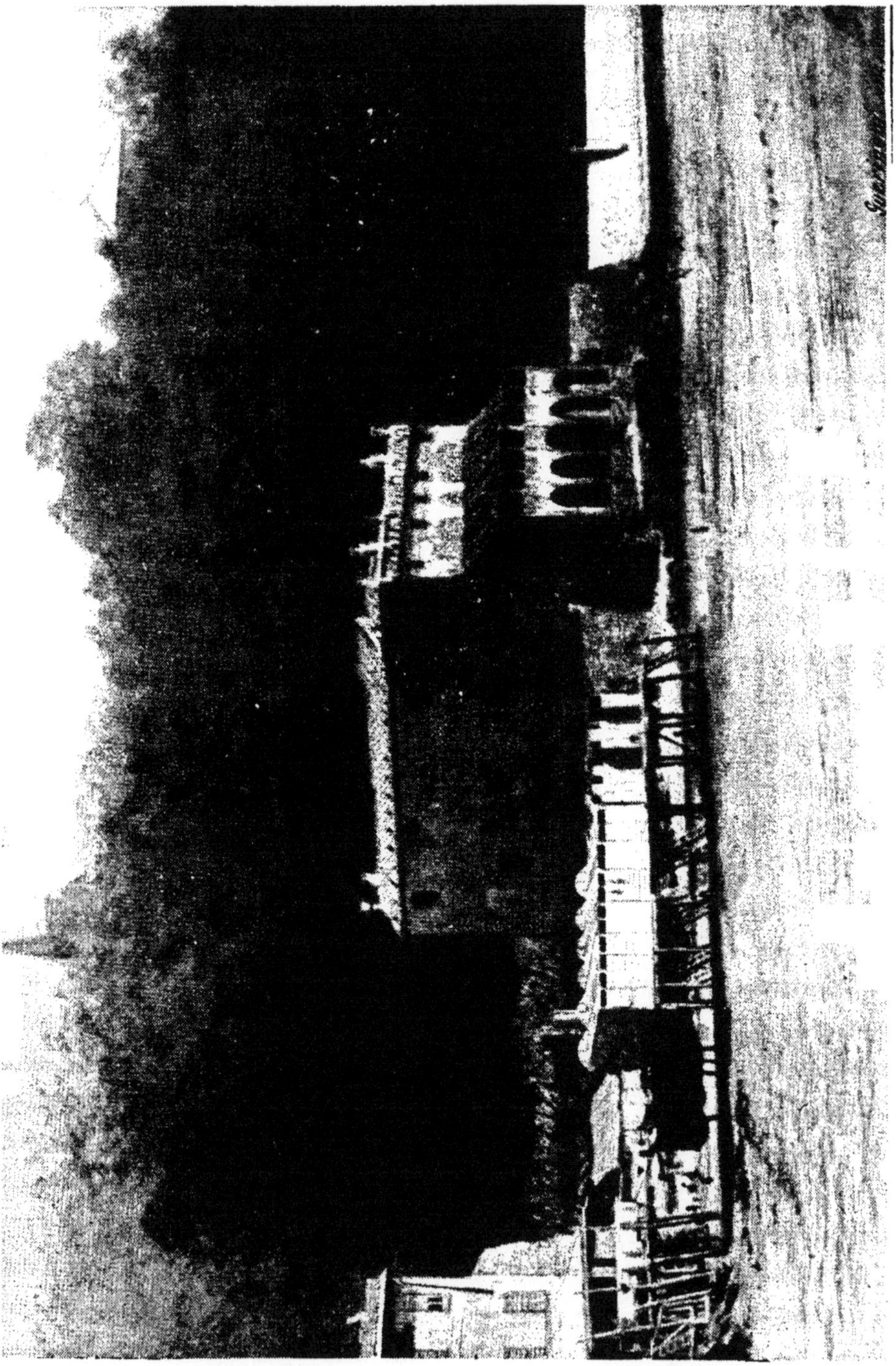

soul ". " I have no words to tell you how I hated that house and the landscape around it. Shelley used to scold me about it. His health was good, and the place suited him exactly. What could I reply to him? That the people were savage and antipathetic, that, notwithstanding the beauty of the position, I should have preferred a place more completely in the country, that housekeeping was very difficult, that our Tuscan servants all wanted to leave us, that the dialect of those Genoese was rough and unpleasant. This was all I could say. I had no words to describe what I felt. The beauty of those woods made me shiver, and feel as if I wanted to cry. So strong was the sense of repulsion

which I felt, that I was content only
when the wind and the waves per-
mitted me to sail out to sea, so that
I might not be forced to take my
usual walk among the trees over
which climbed the luxuriant vines.
Things which I once loved now oppressed me. My only peaceful mo-
ments were those passed on board
that unlucky boat, when, lying with
my head upon his knees, I closed my
eyes and felt only the breath of the
wind and our swift motion ".

The " unlucky boat " had arrived:
from the terrace of Casa Magni there
was seen, on the afternoon of Sunday
the 12th of May, a sail, rounding
the point of Porto Venere. It was
the wished for boat, which Mr

Heslop, with two English sailors, had brought from Genoa to San Terenzo, notwithstanding the rough weather they had experienced, which the boat had borne very well indeed. It measured twenty one feet by eight but looked as if it were twice as large. It had been built after a model that Williams had obtained from one of the royal arsenals in England. It was not covered in, was of solid construction, schooner-rigged with large sails. "We required " writes Trelawney, " two tons of ballast to bring her to her water line, and she bent decidedly before the wind, although she was quite broad enough in the beam ".

The whole crew consisted of an English cabin boy of eighteen, Charles

Vivian, who had come from Genoa with the boat. Trelawney wished that a Genoese sailor acquainted with the coast, should be engaged; but Williams, who considered himself an expert, would not hear of it.

The schooner, when ordered from Captain Roberts at Genoa, was to have been the joint property of Shelley, Trelawney and Williams. Trelawney at that time enthusiastic about Byron, proposed that she should be named " Don Juan " and Shelley did not oppose him. But the idea of partnership was given up before the boat was launched, and she remained Shelley's exclusive property, at the price of 80 pounds sterling (2000 francs). Mary and her poet gave the boat

THE TWO YACHTS "BOLIVAR" AND "DON JUAN".

(From a sketch by E. E. Williams, in the British Museum).

the name of *Ariel:* but Byron nearly flew into 'a rage about it, insisting that the boat should be called after his hero; and ordering Roberts to write the name upon the mainsail. So it arrived, bearing this novel distinction. " For twenty one days and twenty one nights ", writes Mrs. Shelley, " Shelley and Edward discussed whether they should change her name, and wash off the original mark. Turpentine, spirits of wine, lye, all sorts of things were tried for this purpose, but the painted name only faded a little, and that was all. At last we cut the piece out, the boatman mended the sail, and so it was left. I don't know what Lord Byron will say; but noble-

man and poet though he be, we
can't let him turn our craft into a
charcoal boat ".

IV

The days passed by at San Terenzo now sad, now gay. The poet when not writing or conversing, was always at sea. The old priest of the place, a certain De Marchis, told Mantegazza that the sailors themselves often tried to dissuade Shelley from embarking when the sea was high, and danger, was imminent; but he disregarded all advice and continued to live in the element which was to prove his tomb. In fine weather he would leave the house, carrying under his arm the *Sandalino* (that in which Jane embarked for that unique and terrible excursion) made of the fine wood used for the manufacture of sieves and for Nuremburgh boxes, and in this frail shell, more like paper than wood, he dared the waves.

He did not compose much. Lord Byron's society had done him no good. " I have lived too long with Byron, the sun has extinguished the firefly ". His tragedy ' Charles the First ' did not get on; perhaps he experienced the same disgust which hindered Buonarroti from finishing the bust of Brutus, now existing in the ' Tribuna di Michelangelo ' at the Academy of Fine Arts in Florence: the " horror of treason " prevented him from painting Cromwell as a hero. Still, rocked in that fatal boat, culled by the Tyrrhenian waves, amid the mystic splendour of the tranquil sea he wrote the ' Triumph of Life ', the supreme efflorescence of his genius, promising a new manner in his poetry, more serene, more tranquil, more human. " Let us seek truth wherever it may be found. Man's destiny cannot be fallen so low as to believe that he is born only to die ". So he wrote in those last days while meditating the " great mystery " and in the last line of that poem, left, alas, unfinished, he asks:

" Then, what is life? I cried ".

Perhaps he experienced a strange presentiment of his coming end. He asked Trelawney in a letter dated 18th June to procure for him some prussic acid, adding: " I need not say that I have no present idea of killing myself, but I confess it would be a comfort to hold in my hand the golden key of the chamber of eternal rest ".

Meantime Mary had fallen ill, a dangerous miscarriage had brought her almost to death's door. Claire Clairemont who had begun to recover from the shock of Allegra's death, had come from Florence to nurse her. Shelley was tormented by dreams and frightful visions. He thought he saw his own image approaching him and asking him: "Are you satisfied?" Other inhabitants of Casa Magni, also, had strange visions, not at night, but in broad day, and wide awake. Everybody was excited as if they felt themselves on the eve of a catastrophe.

Shelley set off with Williams, on board the *Ariel,* in the direction of Leghorn, on the 1ˢᵗ of July to meet Leigh Hunt. This beloved friend came into Italy (provided by Shelley with funds for the purpose), in order to undertake with Byron the foundation of a literary periodical. The poet had written in dedicating to Hunt his tragedy ' The Cenci ': " Had I known a person more highly endowed than yourself with all that it becomes a man to possess, I had solicited for this work the ornament of his name.

One more gentle, honorable, innocent and brave; one of more exalted toleration for all who do and think evil, and yet himself free from evil; one who knows better how to receive and how to confer a benefit, though he must ever confer far more than he can receive; one of simpler and, in the highest sense of the word, of purer life and manners I never knew; and I had already been fortunate in friendships when your name was added to the list ".

"In that patient and irreconcilable enmity with domestic and political tyranny and imposture', which the tenor of your life has illustrated, and which, had I health and talents, should illustrate mine, let us, comforting each

LEIGH HUNT.

(From the picture by B. R. Haydon in the National
Portrait Gallery. By kind permission of Messrs. Walker
& Boutall, London).

other in our taste, live and die ".
Leigh Hunt was truly the friend of
his heart, *animae dimidium*: he
could hardly realize that he was
really to meet him so soon. On the
afternoon of their departure a fresh
breeze was blowing, which would soon
take them to Leghorn. Williams and
Shelley said Good-bye. Mary was
getting better, and was able to drag
herself as far as the terrace, but she
was terribly depressed, nor could she
reconcile herself to her husband's departure. She was anxious about little
Percy's health. She called Shelley
back two or three times to say that
if she did not see him very soon she
should take the boy to Pisa. She wept
bitterly when they at last started off.

They set sail. At Lerici they met Captain Roberts who boarded the *Ariel,* and that same evening they cast anchor at Leghorn close to Byron's yacht, the *Bolivar,* which had been built for him at the shipyard at Leghorn. They could not get *pratique* that night, so did not disembark until the next morning. At last the two friends met, and Shelley flung himself upon Hunt's neck " and they embraced each other, " Shelley exclaiming " I am inexpressibly delighted – you cannot think how inexpressibly happy it makes me ". Thornton Hunt, Leigh Hunt's eldest son, remembered, many a year later, that greeting and that rapturous cry.

From Leghorn, the Hunts proceeded with Shelley to Pisa, where they were the guests of Byron, who had prepared for them the ground-floor of Palazzo Lanfranchi. Byron was very much displeased at the appearance of Hunt's family, consisting of an invalid wife and seven unruly children. But the incomparable friend did his best to smoothe down the unkindness of the host. He insisted that Doctor Vacca, then one of the ornaments of the Pisan University, should visit the poor woman, to whom he gave but a few months to live. He also did his best to console Hunt for this cruel sentence (which, by the way, was proved not to be correct). He gave him hopes too of Byron's aid in the foundation of the

journal; which certainly hung fire.
It was to have been called 'The
Liberal'. Byron's enthusiasm for it
had greatly waned and he shrank for
the fulfilment of promises, which had
from the first been unwillingly given.
But at last he consented to abandon
the revenues derived from the 'Vi-
sion of Judgment' for the expenses
of the first number of the periodical.
Shelley was divided between hope and
anxiety and wrote mournful letters
to Jane and Mary, lamenting the
bygone hours of the serene intimacy
of Casa Magni, as if he already felt
the presage of disaster. Jane replied
in a letter still more sad, in which
she lamented the delay in the return
of 'Neddy' (her husband), and ending

with the strange postscript: " Why do you speak of not renewing the bygone hours? Are you going to join your friend Plato? ".

They visited the monuments of the city, the Camposanto, the Duomo, the " melancholy leaning Tower, " all the glorious remains of the great past of the Republic. Hunt mentions a talk which they had together. " He approved strongly a remark of mine made in the Cathedral of Pisa while the organ was sounding, namely that there might be a divine religion if it were founded on Charity instead of Faith ". But the hour came for the sad farewell. The truants must return. Williams would not wait, and the two women were panting for their appearance. Leigh Hunt conjured his friend not to venture to sea if the weather were threatening, and gave him, to read on the voyage, a copy of Keat's last volume of poems, containing the sublime fragment called 'Hyperion'.

"Keep it," he said, "until you can give it back to me with your own hand". They exchanged a last embrace, and Shelley's carriage disappeared into the shades of night on the road to Leghorn.

V

The days had been hot, stifling, suffocating: the sun had long reigned triumphant in a sky of brilliant blue, without the hope of even the faintest shadow of a cloud. It was truly the bright sun of Italy with its " pitiless laugh ", so dear to the Poet, but fatal to men, to animals and to the harvest. At Parma the peasants were obliged to break off work in the fields because of the excessive heat, from ten o' clock until five. Water was failing everywhere,

and the priests were imploring heaven
for rain with great pomp of pro-
cessions, uncovering of miraculous
images and carrying about of the
most highly venerated relics.

This could not last. On the
8th July, the fatal monday, the long
desired rain seemed approaching. The
aspect of the sky was changed; a
tempest broke out, but it remained
distant, and the serenity of the sky
returned. Shelley spent the whole
morning in visiting the bank, and
laying in provisions for the colony at
Casa Magni. Then, always accompanied by Trelawney, he returned to
the port. A light breeze was setting
in the direction of Lerici, and
Williams, who was in a hurry to get

off, declared that in seven hours they would arrive. Shelley had been, that morning, in very high spirits, as sometimes happens when some obscure danger threatens. He would not listen to the predictions of Captain Roberts who continued to declare that a violent hurricane was imminent.

By noon or soon after, the two friends, with Charles Vivian, were on board the *Ariel*. Trelawney wished to accompany them out to sea in the *Bolivar,* of which he had the command, but was prevented by sanitary formalities. Between one and two, the Ariel left the harbour, almost in the company of two feluccas, while Trelawney, grim and frowning, un-

willingly ordered the sails of the
Bolivar to be furled, and her anchor
to be let go. With a double spyglass he watched the boat with his two
friends, following its movements with
an anxious eye. " They should have
left earlier this morning, " said the
genoese pilot of the *Bolivar,* adding:
"They keep too close to the shore, the
current will catch them ". " They
will soon have a breeze off shore, "
answered Trelawney. " Perhaps, "
answered the pilot. " They will soon
have a fresh breeze. It is mad to
hoist that sail on an open boat, that
has no real sailor aboard of her ".
Then turning to the south east he
said: " Look at those black lines and
spots of cloud just there over them

— look how the water smokes. —
The devil is putting his tail into
things ". Captain Roberts, too, from
the end of the wharf, was watching
the *Ariel*. He saw her, going at first
with a velocity of seven knots an
hour, then, mounting to the top of
the linghthouse, which dominated a
vast extent of sea, he saw with terror
the hurricane advancing from the
gulf and wrapping in its folds the
fragile bark, of which the mainsail
had been lowered. " In the darkness
of the hurricane, " he said, " it was
hidden from my gaze, I could distin-
guish it no longer. When the storm
had subsided a little, I looked for it
once more, looked again and again,
hoping that it might reappear; but

on the whole expanse of sea, there was not a single boat ".

Meanwhile Trelawney, over-powered by the heat, had gone down into the cabin a prey to irresistible drowsiness. He was awakened by a great noise on deck, the sailors were letting down another anchor to ensure the *Bolivar* from bursting loose. In the harbour there was a great confusion. There were loud cries on all sides, as if the end of the world had come, everybody was seeking shelter from the tempest. It was six o'clock, or perhaps a little after, but it was already dark: the sea being of a dark leaden colour looked as if covered by an oily scum. Furious gusts of wind were succeeded by incessant thunder and lightning and it poured in torrents. The full violence of the storm lasted about twenty minutes. When the sky began to lighten a little, Trelawney looked towards every point of the horizon, seeking for the *Ariel,* hoping that in some way or other she might have been saved. At eight o'clock he went on shore, but the storm continued all night. At dawn he returned to the *Bolivar* to see if there were any news. Nobody knew anything. " My Genoese, with his lynx eyes, had caught sight on board one of the fishing boats an English oar which he believed that he had seen on board Shelley's schooner, but the whole crew swore by all the saints in the calendar that it was nothing of the kind ".

Agonizing hours passed and days of agony: on the morning of the third day, Trelawney went to Pisa, and flew to Palazzo Lanfranchi, hoping to find a letter with news from Casa Magni. Nothing! " I told my fears to Hunt, " he writes, " and then went upstairs to Byron. When I told him, his lips quivered and his voice faltered as he questioned me. I sent a Courier to Leghorn to despatch the *Bolivar* to cruise along the coast, while I mounted my horse and rode in the same direction. I also despat_ched a courier along the road, orde_ring him to go as far as Nice ".

VI

During those days the two poor widows at Casa Magni had been in the most cruel anxiety.

Mary was slowly recovering, but was oppressed by such invincible melancholy that she was almost always in tears. For her mother-heart these summer days were full of agonizing memories. Three years before, on a hot day in June, she had seen the shade of death creep over the blue eyes of William, her beautiful boy, who seemed to beckon to her from his green grave in the cemetery beside the pyramid of Caius Cestus at Rome. Now she trembled for her little Percy, on whom she lavished all her affection. Shelley's return was longed for as for a healing balsam. He had written to Mary once or twice describing the difficulties he had encountered in the arrangement of Hunt's affairs, adding that he could not say when he should arrive. Thus a week passed. On Monday the 8.th, Jane received a letter from Edward dated Saturday, saying that he was waiting at Leghorn for Shelley, who had been detained at Pisa. Shelley would be sure to return, but he wrote that, if on Monday he had not arrived, he should embark in a felucca and would be with them by Tuesday at the latest.

" This was Monday, the fatal Monday, " writes the desolate widow in her letter to Mrs. Gisborne. " But with us it was stormy all day, and we could not believe that they had put to sea. At twelve at night we had a thunder-storm. On Tuesday it rained all day and the sea was calm; the sky wept over their graves. On Wednesday the wind was fair from Leghorn and several feluccas arrived thence. One brought word that they had sailed on Monday, but we did not believe them. Thursday was another day of fair wind, and when twelve at night came, and we did not see the tall sails of the little boat double the promontory before us, we began to fear, not the truth, but some illness, some unpleasant cause for their detention ". Poor women! They still cherished illusions.

"Jane got so uneasy, that she determined to proceed next day to Leghorn in a boat, to see what was the matter. Friday came, and with it a heavy sea and adverse wind. Jane, however, resolved to be rowed to Leghorn, since no boat could sail, and passed the day in preparations for the voyage. I wished her to wait for letters, since Friday was post day. She did not wish to, but the sea detained her; the swell rose so that no boat would venture out. At twelve at noon our letters came. There was one from Hunt to Shelley, saying : " Pray, tell us how you fared on Monday ". And " we are anxious ". The paper fell from my hands. I trembled all over. Jane read it. " Then it is all over, " she said. " No, my dear Jane, it is not all over, " I cried, " but this suspense is dreadful. Come with me; we will go to Leghorn. We will post, and be swift to learn our fate. We tried to encourage each other, but death was in our hearts. We crossed to Lerici, despair in our hearts. They raised our spirits there, by telling us that no accident had been heard of, that it must have been known, etc. But still our fear was great, and without resting we posted to Pisa.

It must have been fearful to see us, two poor, wild, aghast creatures, driving towards the sea to learn if we were to be for ever doomed to misery ". Truly a sad and pitiful sight! " I knew that Hunt was at Pisa in Lord Byron's house, but I thought that Byron was at Leghorn. We settled to drive to Casa Lanfranchi, where I was to get out, and ask of Hunt the terrible question: ' Do you know anything of Shelley?' On entering Pisa the idea of seeing Hunt for the first time after four years, and asking him such a question, was so terrible to me that I could hardly prevent myself from going into convulsions. My efforts after calm were immense. I knocked at the

door, some one called out: " Who 's
there?" It was the Guiccioli's maid.
Byron was at Pisa. Hunt was in bed,
so I was to see Lord Byron instead
of him. This was a great relief to me.
I staggered upstairs; the Guiccioli
came forward smiling to meet me,
while I could scarcely say: " Where
is he? Do you know anything of
Shelley?" She knew nothing; he had
left Pisa on Sunday; on Monday he
had sailed; there had been bad
weather on Monday afternoon; more
they knew not. " Both Lord Byron
and the Countess have told me since,
that on that terrible evening I looked
more like a ghost than a woman;
light seemed to emanate from my
features, my face was white as

marble ". *Ed ella era di pietra,* and
she was of marble, like the Lady of
whom Leopardi sang, who walks
alone to meet the storm and wind.
" Alas! " she goes on, " I had risen
from a bed of sickness for this
journey. I had travelled all day; it
was now twelve at night, and we,
refusing rest, proceeded to Leghorn,
not in despair; no, for then we must
have died, but with sufficient hope
to buoy up the agitation of spirits
which was all my life. It was past
two in the morning when we arrived. They took us to the wrong
inn; neither Trelawney nor Captain
Roberts was there, so we were
obliged to wait until daylight. We
threw ourselves dressed on our beds,

and slept a little, but at six o' clock we went out to ask at one or two inns for one or the other of these gentlemen. We found Roberts at the *Globe.* He came down to us with a face which seemed to assure us of the worst; and here we learned all that had occurred during the week they had been absent from us, and under what circumstances they had started on their return ".

There still remained a thread of hope. The boat might have been driven by the tempest on the coast of Corsica or Elba. It had been seen, it was said, in the gulf. Who could tell? " We resolved to return, " continues Mrs Shelley, " with all possible speed. We sent a courier, to

go from tower to tower along the
coast, to learn if anything had been
seen or found; and at 9 a. m. we
quitted Leghorn, stopped but one
moment at Pisa and proceeded
towards Lerici. When two miles
from Viareggio, we rode down to
that town to hear if they knew
anything. Here our calamity first
began to break upon us. A little
boat and a water cask had been
found five miles off. (They had built
themselves a tiny canoe in " order to
land without getting wet, because our
boat drew four feet of water ". It was
the wellknown *sandalino* in which
Jane had heard Shelley's strange
question about the great mystery).

" The description, " writes Mary

" tallies with that of the little boat they had made, but then that boat was very cumbersome, and in bad weather they might easily be led to throw it overboard. The cask frightened me more, but the same reason might in some sort be given for that ".

Truly a sad, a horrible journey! The two poor women sought every pretext for delaying to give way to the awful doubts which tormented them. Certainly Trelawney, who was with them, did his best to delude them with pious falsehoods.

" We journeyed on, and reached the Magra at about half past ten p. m. I cannot describe to you what I felt when, in fording the river, I first felt the water splash about the wheels. I was suffocated. I gasped for breath. I thought I should have gone into convulsions, and I struggled that Jane might not perceive it. Looking down the river, I saw two great lights burning at the Foce. A voice within me seemed to cry aloud: " There is his grave! "

" After passing the river, I gradually recovered. Arriving at Lerici, we were obliged to cross our little bay in a boat. San Terenzo was illuminated for a festa. What a scene! The rolling sea, the scirocco wind, the lights of the town towards which we rowed, and our desolate hearts that shadowed all as if with a shroud. We landed; nothing had been heard of them. This was Saturday July 13th, and thus we waited until Thursday July 18th, tossed about by hope and fear. We sent messengers along the coast towards Genoa and to Viareggio; nothing had been found but the skiff. Reports were brought us; we hoped — and yet, to tell you all the agony we endured during those six days would be to make you conceive a universe of pain, each moment intolerable, and giving place to one still worse. The people of the country, too, added to our discomfort; they were like wild savages. On *festas* the men and women and children, in bands, the sexes always separate, pass the whole night in dancing on the sands, close to our door, running into the sea, then back again, all the time yelling one detestable air at the top of their voices — the most detestable in the world. Then the scirocco blew perpetually, and the sea forever moaned their dirge.

"On Thursday, the 18th, Trelawney left us, to go to Leghorn to see what was doing, or could be done. On Friday 19th, I was very ill: but as evening came on, I said to Jane: "If anything had been found on the coast, Trelawney would have returned to let us know. He has not returned, so I still hope. At about 7 o' clock p. m. he did return. All was over: all was quiet now. They had been found, washed on shore ".

Such is the unhappy Mary's

description of these days, written who can tell with what pangs and tears? Perhaps it was not altogether painful to gather up the memories of those hours, which had seemed to her ages of martyrdom, and were the beginning of her widowhood. For her life had no more delight, no more purpose. She had outlived the best and dearest portion of herself. Resignation olny was left. Sad consolation to those who have no other.

Upon Trelawney, the friend of those terrible hours, to whom were left the last sad offices of friendship, devolved also the painful and difficult duty of announcing to the two ladies that their misfortune was certain and irreparable.

He returned to Casa Magni, once more beholding those scenes which had witnessed so many happy hours. On the threshold of the sorrow-stricken dwelling, he paused as if in a dream. He started, as Caterina, the baby's nurse, came out to meet him. Scarcely answering her, he passed up the stairs and entered unannounced. " I spoke not, nor did they question me. Mrs. Shelley's large grey eyes were fixed upon my face. I turned away. Incapable of enduring this terrible silence she exclaimed: ' Then there is no longer any hope? ' I did not answer but left the room and sent to them the maid with the children ". A gentle, a truly human thought. It seems like the close of a tragedy.

On the next day, July 20th, he himself accompanied to Pisa the two women, that they might not be tormented by the sight of the fatal sea, that they might be consoled by Hunt's company, and that Trelawney might hasten the completion of the pious offices which he had undertaken. Mary remembered that " slope of green access, where, like an infant's smile over the dead, a light of laughing flowers along the grass is spread[1] ".

She recalled the verdant cemetery in Rome, near the Pyramid of Caius Cestius, where little William had been laid to rest, and where stood the

---

[1] Adonais. XLIX.

tomb of Keats. It was decided that
Shelley's body should be taken
to Rome, and that of Williams
transported to England.

Nothing was left to the two
widows but their tears. " To-day, "
writes Mrs. Shelley, " the sun is
shining brightly, Hunt, Lord Byron
and Trelawney have gone to that
desolate shore, to render the last
offices to their remains. The quarantine laws forbid that they should
be reburied, and exact that they shall
be burnt. I do not dislike the idea.
His ashes shall be placed in Rome
beside those of my boy, and one day
mine, too, shall join them there.
Adonais is not Keats' elegy, it is his
very own. In it he calls us to follow

MONUMENT TO KEATS AT ROME.

M. e S. Firenze

him to Rome. I have seen the spot where he lies, the pine trunks that mark the place where the sand covers him. But they will not burn him there. *It is too near Viareggio.* At this moment they are occupied in this terrible office — and I still live ".

VII

Wrapped in the austere mantle of their grief, the two victims of the terrible drama which we here recount, with the aid of documents already published, vanish from our pages. Now follows the epilogue for which we have obtained fresh evidence, hitherto entirely unknown, gathered from the archives of Florence, of Lucca, and of Leghorn, and *viva voce* from certain old sailors at Viareggio, who were present at the discovery and the cremation of

Shelley's remains, and at the recovery of the *Ariel.*

Trelawney and Mary both write that there had been found at Viareggio, two days later than that of the disaster the well–known skiff, a trunk or cask, and some bottles, which had undoubtedly belonged to the unhappy *Ariel.*

Trelawney, after accompanying the two women to Casa Magni, continued his researches in that vicinity. He had interested the sanitary guards in his object, by the promise of an important sum of money in case of success. Every morning, very early, two dragoons of the Duke of Lucca's Guard, were to regularly patrol the shore, observing whatever was worthy of notice, and making written reports to the Captain in command of the Sanitary station at the Foce. They were to register everything, the direction of the wind, the aspect of the sky and the sea. Certainly they must have noted on the 18th of July the event which was announced to the Minister of Foreign and Internal Affairs of Lucca by the Governor of Viareggio, in the letter which we give below; but unfortunately we have been unable to find these registers of the Sanitary guard, either at the *Capitaneria* of the port of Viareggio, or in the Archives of Lucca.

The letter is as follows:

(Royal Archives at Lucca. Foreign Affairs. Year 1822).

381.

N.º 89. Duchy of Lucca.

Viareggio, July 18th 1822.

The Counsellor of State. Governor of the City of Viareggio. President of the Sanitary Committee. To his Excellency the Minister for Home and Foreign affairs.

Lucca.

" Your Excellency,

It is my duty to inform you that to-day the sea which has been rather rough has washed up a body in an advanced state of decay, and that the said body has, after due inspection by the Sanitary Tribunal been interred upon the beach, covered according to the Sanitary regulations now in force, with strong lime.

We have had no information respecting the same, but it is believed to be one of the young Englishmen who were said to have suffered shipwreck during a voyage undertaken by a small boat shaped like a brig, which left Leghorn for the gulf of Spezia on the 8th July, the other having been cast by the heavy sea on the Tuscan Coast.

Receive your Excellency the expression etc. etc.

The Governor above mentioned

G. P. FREDIANI.

P. S. What leads me more

especially to believe that it may be one of the said two Englishmen, is that an English book has been found in the pocket of a double-breasted jacket of mixed cloth, such as he always wore. The rest of his attire consisted of a pair of nankeen trowsers from Malta, and a pair of boots with white silk socks underneath, the whole of which have been buried, according to existing regulations ".

This document is not without interest and importance. It proves to us that the body of Shelley was *straccato*, i. e. washed up, on the beach at Viareggio, precisely on the 18th July while that of Williams, since Governor Frediani had already had notice of it, must have been cast up earlier on the Tuscan coast. We also learn what coat the poet was wearing, and there can be no doubt concerning the " English book, " it having been the volume of Keats which Leigh Hunt had lent to his friend, " turned down " at the *Eve of St Agnes* " as if the reader, in the act of reading had hastily thrust it away ".

Trelawney stopped at Viareggio in time to see the corpse before its burial. " The face, the hands and such parts of the body as were unprotected by the dress, were fleshless. That tall, slight figure, the jacket, the volume of Sophocles in one pocket, of Keats in the other, were things too familiar to me to leave any doubt that this mutilated corpse was that

M. e S. Firenze

THE "SOPHOCLES" TAKEN FROM SHELLEY'S DEAD HAND

of Shelley,[1] Williams' body had washed up three miles further south, on Tuscan territory, near to Tower of Migliarino, at the mouth of the Serchio. The faithful friend hastened at once to identify it, proceeding to the place which he calls in his *Recollections* " Bocca Lericcio, " an inappropriate and unknown name. " This corpse was even more mutilated; it had no other clothing than the fragments of a shirt, partly pulled over the head as if the wearer had been in the act of taking it off, a black silk scarf, knotted round the neck as sailors wear them, socks,

---

[1] It was a volume of .*Sophocles,* and not of *Aeschylus,* as Trelawney wrote erroneously afterwards. The precious volume is now preserved in the Bodleian Library, at Oxford.

and one shoe; showing that he was in the act of taking off his clothes. The flesh, sinews and muscles hung in strips like the shirt, showing the bones, and the ribs. I had brought with me from Casa Magni one of Williams' shoes, which matched in size exactly the one which the corpse still had on. This shoe, and the black scarf, assured me that the body was that of Shelley 's companion. Williams was the only one of the three who could swim and was probably the last to perish. It is also probable that as he was better dressed than the others and had upon him a watch and some money, that his body may have been robbed before it was discovered ".

It is exceedingly probable that Shelley had perished without an attempt to save himself, in order not to imperil the life of one who might strive to save him. As to the sailor-boy, Charles Vivian, we know from a letter of Captain Domenico Simoncini, Sanitary officer at Viareggio, published by Trelawney, that on that same day, July 18th and not " three weeks after the ship-wreck ", as he writes, there was thrown up on the shore at Massa a corpse, without the head, which had been eaten by fishes. It had on a cotton jacket and a pair of blue and white striped trowsers, and was barefooted. This body was burnt on the spot where it was found, and the ashes were buried in the sand. These were, no doubt, the mortal remains of the third victim of the shipwreck of the *Ariel*.

The two bodies having been recognized, were temporarily buried where they had been found; it was now necessary to discover some means of transferring them to some place of honorable sepulture. Trelawney applied to Mr. Dawkins, then English Resident at Florence, and Chargé d' Affaires near the Duke of Lucca. Dawkins wrote from the Baths of Lucca (where he was then staying) to Trelawney the letter published by the latter, advising him to ask only for permission to convey Shelley's remains to Leghorn.

Having obtained such a permission and procured the necessary papers, he would be able to convey the body, by sea or land, wherever he pleased. With regard to the other body, that of Williams, an answer from Florence was awaited. Dawkins had despatched, without delay, to Mansi, Home and Foreign Secretary to the Duke of Lucca, the following *Memorandum* (Written in French).

(Royal State Archives of Lucca. Foreign Affairs, 1822).

381.

" A small Brigantine the property of Mr. Shelley, an English gentleman, sank, near the mouth of the Serchio, last week. The crew consisted of three individuals, namely: Mr. Shelley, Captain Williams, of the British Army, and an English sailor-boy. The remains of the first two have been washed up by the sea on the coast of Lucca, the second on that of Tuscany. Mr. Shelleys's relations and friends wish to remove his remains from the spot where they are now buried to the English cemetery at Leghorn ".

Mansi, who thus annotates this letter " This document I received from the hand of Mr. Dawkins, British Chargé d'Affaires, " writes as follows, to the Governor of the town of Viareggio.

383.

To His Excellency the Governor
of the town of Viareggio.

Lucca, 27th July 1822.

" Excellency,

The British Legation accredited
to this Court has apprised me that
a small Brigantine belonging to
Mr. Shelley an English gentleman,
was wrecked some days ago, near
the mouth of the Serchio. Three
persons were on board the said
vessel, namely, Mr. Shelley (the
owner) Captain Williams of H. B. M.'s
service, and a young English sailor,
and that the bodies of the first two
have been cast on shore, that of
Captain Williams on the coast of

Tuscany, that of Mr. Shelley on the coast of this Duchy. Further, the above-mentioned Legation, having represented to me that the relatives of the late Mr. Shelley desired to remove his mortal remains from the place where they were buried to the English cemetery at Leghorn, urgently press me to obtain from this Government the necessary orders for the exhumation of the said body and for its removal from this Duchy.

The above statements appear to leave no doubt that the corpse before-mentioned is the same which is alluded to in your Excellency's esteemed Dispatch of the 18th inst., marked N.° 89.

His Majesty having granted the

request preferred by the English Legation, it devolves upon me to beg your Excellency to be pleased to grant the necessary dispensations in order that the body of the late Englishman, buried upon this coast be given to the person duly authorized, who shall present himself to your Excellency for that purpose.

It is of course clearly understood that the sanitary laws in force must be duly observed in their entirety by the persons in question. The removal of the body will most probably be effected by sea, and all the expense incurred in the execution of the transport, must be borne by the Person charged with the reception of the consignment of the body.

I take this opportunity to assure your Excellency that etc. etc. ".

Meantime negotiations were proceeding, at first confidentially, with the Tuscan Government, for the exhumation of the remains of Williams. Dawkins, partly to oblige a friend of Lord Byron's, but even more for a zealous sense of duty, which made him write — " Do not mention trouble, I am here to take as much as my countrymen see fit to give me, " had written either on the 25th or 26th July to Don Neri Corsini, Minister of Foreign Affairs to the Grand Duke; who sends the following official communication to the "President of Good Government, " that is the Police Minister:

(*State Archives of Florence.
Foreign Affairs Prot. 95: N.° 63*).

To the Hon. President
  of Good Government.

27th July 1822.

" Illustrious Sir,

The Royal Legation of Great Britain informs me that Captain Williams having been drowned last week in the vicinity of the mouth of the river Serchio, and buried in a neighbouring field, which, we are assured, is Tuscan territory, the Legation earnestly requests that the body of the said Officer may be exhumed and conveyed to the English Cemetery at Leghorn. The Imperial and Royal Government not considering it desirable to refuse this request, it being understood that the exhumation is to be conducted according to the tenor of the regulations, I am charged to entreat your Illustrious Lordship to give such orders as you judge expedient, either to the Magistrate or the local Authorities in the jurisdiction where the aforesaid corpse has been interred, as well as to the Government of Leghorn; and to apprise me approximately when your instructions and authorizations can reach the above named magistrates or authorities in order that through the British Legation, the necessary information may be conveyed to two English Gentlemen who will proceed to the place in question to be present at the disinterment, and will defray all expenses consequent thereupon.

I avail myself, etc. etc. ".

Everything appeared to be going smoothly, thanks to the goodwill of the Tuscan Government. Dawkins' request, we must remember, spoke only of the disinterment of the bodies, and their removal to the English Cemetery at Leghorn. He had preferred the same request at Lucca and at Florence, and it had seemed to be favourably received; but there intervened a prolonged interchange of documents between the various offices concerned in the affair. The " President of Good Government " wrote, accordingly, to Spannocchi Governor of Leghorn, apprising him that he had given instructions to the Auditor of the Government of Pisa to attend to the disinterment of the corpse of Captain Williams. And Spannocchi, immediately warned the Auditor of Pisa that he had made the necessary arrangements with the Reverend Mr. Hall, pastor of the English Church at Leghorn. But the Auditor replied that the Commander of the Fort at the mouth of the Serchio would not permit the disinterment of the remains, still less their transportation, since the then existing sanitary laws which appear to have been so strict as to be almost ridiculous, did not allow of anything of the kind. " The corpse in question was cast up from the sea, disfigured and in a state of putrefaction, was not known, nor recognized as that of Williams, nor is it known whether Williams or the person to whom the corpse belonged had, in the sea, meeting or communication, before or after death. Consequently it does not seem possible that we can allow from a sanitary point of view, either the exhumation or the removal of the above–mentioned corpse ".[1]

The Police Minister (or President of Good Government) Aurelio Puccini was apprised of these difficulties by a letter from the Secretary

---

[1] These documents exist in the Archives of the R. Prefecture at Leghorn.

of the Governor of Leghorn dated
31st July.

It became necessary to apply to
His Excellency the Imperial and
Royal Secretary of State, Superintendent of the Sanitary Department,
who was precisely that same Prince
Neri Corsini, who was Minister of
Foreign Affairs, who had probably
sent for Dawkins in order to arrange
this affair. At this point and not
sooner, was broached the idea following, " to avoid the obstacles in-
terposed by the sanitary laws, the
ancient custom of burning bodies of
the dead to ashes. " Certainly it was
at that period that the first request
was recalled and replaced by the
following one, bearing a date much

later than that of the negotiations already entered into on the subject, with the Tuscan Government.

(*State Archives of Florence. Foreign Affairs. Prot. 95, N.º 63*).

To His Excellency,
Prince Corsini, etc. etc.

" Prince,

Two English gentlemen, Captain Williams and Mr. Shelley embarked on the 12th of last month at Leghorn to rejoin their families at Spezia. Surprised by the storm which took place on the following day, their vessel, the property of Mr. Shelley, sank with all on board, consisting of the above-mentioned gentlemen, and a young English sailor.

" The remains of the Captain were cast on the 17th July on Tuscan territory, those of Mr. Shelley on that of Lucca, near the mouth of the Serchio. The relatives of Captain Williams have requested me to obtain permission from the Tuscan Government to transport his corpse, or at least his ashes, from the spot where they have been interred to the Cemetery at Leghorn, with a view to their removal to England.

" I have had the honour of addressing a similar request on the part of the family of Mr. Shelley to the Government of H. M. the Duchess of Lucca, who has granted the permission.

I avail myself, etc. etc.

G. DAWKINS ".

This application, where there appear besides certain (french) orthographical errors, those mistakes concerning the place and the date of the disaster, which have been perpetuated in all, even the most correct of the biographies of Shelley, was dispatched to the Governor of Leghorn , for the necessary information. And he replied, in the following official terms.

(Archives of State, Florence. Foreign Affairs. Prot. 95. N.° 63).

To H. E. Counselor Corsini
    Superintendent Sanitary
    Department
        Florence.

" Your Excellency,

The request preferred by this British Legation to be allowed to cause to be burned (with all sanitary precautions) the body, known to be that of Captain Williams, already interred on the coast at Migliarino, in order that the ashes may be conveyed to this Protestant Cemetery, can encounter no opposition, provided the said operation, (which is prescribed by our Regulations for such tracts of shore as are composed not of dry land but of rock, or shifting sand) be executed with all necessary sanitary precautions.

" Having consulted our Medical Officer of Health, Cavaliere Palloni, I am therefore of opinion that the exhumation and succeeding cremation of the above-mentioned corpse, may take place on the spot where it has already been interred; and, in order that, on such an occasion all those prescriptions contained in the existing orders, shall be carefully observed, I propose to send to the spot one of our most skilful and trustworthy health-officers, with all necessary instructions, that the operation in question may be carried out with the utmost regularity.

" This much I have the honour to submit to your Excellency, in reply to your most esteemed Dispatch, dated yesterday and, awaiting your further pleasure on the subject, I have the honour to inscribe myself etc. etc.

From the Imperial and Royal Sanitary Secretariat, Leghorn.... August 1822.

SPANNOCCHI ".

Now that it had been decided to cremate the body immediately upon its exhumation, no further obstacle remained. It was simply necessary to inform the " Signori Inglesi " that the expenses of the operation would fall upon them, and that they must make appropriate arrangements with the Governor of Leghorn. Prince Corsini apprised Mr. Dawkins of these facts on the third of August by means of the following letter written in a French, which really should have been put in quarantine.

(*State Archives, Florence. Foreign Affairs. Prot. 95. N.° 63.*

To Mr. Dawkins.

3 August 1833.

" Sir,

The Sanitary Magistrate of Leghorn puts no difficulty in the way of the disinterment and burning of the body of the late Captain Williams buried in a point on the coast of Migliarino, saving all the precautions ordered by the laws (*Loix*) in such cases, for the ashes to be afterwards transported in the Cemetery of the Protestants at Leghorn.

" While hastening to bring this result to your knowledge, I have also the honour to inform you that the

English Gentlemen interested that this operation should be effected, and at whose charge all the relative expenses will lie, will have to address themselves to His Excellency the Governor of Leghorn — charged to give the necessary orders, in order that all should be strictly executed after Sanitary Regulations.

" I take the opportunity etc. etc.

In the same Protocol of the Ministry of Foreign Affairs whence we take these letters, we find one more document. It is a " Memorial for the Royal Secretariat for Foreign Affairs " in the handwriting of His Excellency the Prince Don Neri Corsini, as Head of the Department of State. In it the Minister of Foreign Affairs is recommended to notify to the English Legation the result of the affair, exhorting him to arrange for its execution with the Governor of Leghorn. But the Tuscan Minister of Foreign Affairs, the Head of the Department of State, and the Sanitary Superintendent, were three persons in one sole Prince Don Neri Corsini! Nor was this all! The Memorial is dated August the 8th, while the letter to Dawkins which we have given, already written by the same Corsini is dated the 3rd. Men worthy of Plutarch's Lives, these Tuscan Ministers!

VIII

The necessary permission having been, thanks to the effectual intervention of Dawkins, obtained, both at Lucca and at Florence, Trelawney set about preparing for the completion of the kindly office which had been confided to him. He procured at Leghorn a sheet-iron furnace of the dimensions of a human body, and an abundant provision of fuel. He took with him, besides, two small oaken cases which had been constructed on purpose, lined inside with black

ARD WYNDHAM HARRINGTON SCHENLEY.

(BORN 1800, DIED 1878).

velvet, and bearing on each lid, a metal shield on which was engraved in Latin, the name, age and country of the deceased.

On the 14th August, Trelawney with an English friend of his, Captain Shenley, set sail from Leghorn in the *Bolivar* having promised Hunt and Byron that they should be apprised in time to arrive at the spot as soon as everything was ready. The breeze being light and uncertain, they passed ten or eleven hours on the journey. Casting anchor and disembarking, they made arrangements with the Commandant of the Fort at Bocca del Serchio.[1]

---

[1] This is the real name of the Fort which Trelawney usually calls " The Tower of Migliarino, at the Bocca Lericcio ".

This officer had already received the necessary instruction from the Tuscan Government, and the cremation was fixed for the day following, at noon, Byron being of it informed by a messenger.

On the morning after, Trelawney as he writes in his *Recollections*, received a letter from Byron, assuring him that he would come if possible at a little before the hour fixed. " At ten we went on board the Commandant's boat, with a Squadron of soldiers in fatigue dress, armed with spades and mattocks as well as an officer of health with several of his men ".

Owing to the prevailing terror of contagion by which sanitary regulations were at that period inspired, " they had certain toots so fashioned that the necessary work could be performed without requiring any personal contact with objects which might be infected — that is to say, tongs with long handles, pincers, poles with hooks, spikes of iron and divers other implements which gave one an idea of the instruments of torture used by the Holy Inquisition. Thus armed, we set off, followed by my boat with the furnace and other things which I had brought from Leghorn, " said to have been such as were used by Shelley's beloved Greeks, at their funereal pyres. " We coasted along for some distance landing where a line of

strong posts and railings pointed out
the boundary between the States of
Tuscany and of Lucca. We walked
along the beach to the grave, where
we were soon joined by Byron and
Hunt. They too, had with them an
officer with some soldiers from Migliarino, an officer from the Health
Office, and a few dismounted dragoons,
so that we were surrounded by
soldiers, who kept the ground clear
and spontaneously offered their
assistance. There was a considerable
assemblage of spectators collected
from the vicinity, among them some
ladies very richly dressed. The spot
where the body lay was marked by
the gnarled trunk of a pine tree ".

" A rough cabin, built of pine logs,

covered with branches of the same tree, to keep out the rain and sun, and thatched with reeds, stood on the beach as a shelter for the lookout men on duty. A few yards from this was the grave, which they began to uncover, the gulfs of Spezia and Leghorn being at about equal distances from us. As to fuel, I might have saved myself the trouble of bringing any, for there was an ample supply of broken spars and planks cast on shore from wrecks, besides the fallen and decaying timber in a stunted pine forest close at hand. The soldiers collected fuel whilst I erected the furnace, and then the men of the Health Office set to work shovelling away the sand which covered the

body , while we gathered round
watching anxiously. The first indi-
cation of their having found the body
was the appearance of the end of a
black silk kerchief. I grubbed this
out with a stick, for we were not
allowed to touch anything with our
hands. Then some shreds of linen
were met with, and a boot with the
bone of the leg and the foot in
it. On the removal of a layer of
brushwood, all that now remained of
my lost friend was exposed — a
shapeless mass of bones and flesh.
The limbs separated from the trunk
on being touched ".

Here Byron stepped forward, with
a gesture which recalled that of
Hamlet when the grave‑diggers

spade turns up the shining skull of Yorick:

" Is that a human body!" exclaimed Byron, " why it 's more like the carcass of a sheep, or any other animal, than a man: this is a satire on our pride and folly ".

But it was an inopportune moment for such reflexions. And Trelawney who rather seems to enjoy describing the lugubrious scene, with a certain tinge of romance, goes on: " I pointed to the letters E. E. W. on the black silk handkerchief. Byron looking on, muttered, ' The entrails of a worm hold together longer than the potter 's clay, of which man is made. Hold! let me see the jaw ', he added, as they were removing the skull, ' I can recognize any one by the teeth, with whom I have talked. I always watch the lips and mouth; they tell what tongue and eyes try to conceal '.

But Trelawney had a more practical notion of recognition. " I had a boot of Williams' with me: it exactly corresponded with the one found in the grave. The remains were removed piecemeal into the furnace ".

" Don't repead this with me, " said Lord Byron. " Let my carcass rot where it falls ".

" The funeral pyre was now ready. I applied the fire, and the materials being dry and resinous, the pine-wood burnt furiously, and drove us back. It was hot enough before, there was no breath of air, and the loose sand scorched our feet. As soon as the flames became clear, and allowed us to approach, we threw frankincense and salt into the furnace, and poured a flask of wine and oil over the body. The Greek oration was omitted, for we had lost our Hellenic bard. It was now so insufferably hot that the officers and soldiers were all seeking shade ".

Here Byron made an audacious proposal. " Let us try the strength of these waters that drowned our friends. How far out do you think they were when their boat sank ? "

" If you don' t wish to be put into the furnace, you had better not try. You are not in condition, " said I.

Useless advice! He stripped and plunged into the sea, followed by Trelawney and by Shenley. However, after swimming out a mile, Byron felt tired and turned back to land. Shenley, siezed with cramp, did the same with Trelawney 's assistance.

" At four o' clock, " Trelawney continues, " the funeral pyre burnt low, and when we uncovered the furnace nothing remained in it but dark-coloured ashes, with fragments of the larger bones. Poles were now put under the red-hot furnace, and it was gradually cooled in the sea. I gathered together the human ashes,

and placed them in a small oak-box
bearing an inscription on a brass
plate, screwed it down and placed it
in Byron 's carriage ".

Byron and Hunt returned to Pisa
promising to be at Viareggio the
next day, while Trelawney, with his
escort, retraced the road over which
they had passed that morning, dining
and sleeping at the tavern at Bocca
di Serchio.

Next day, with the same implements (but certainly not " with the
same party " as he writes, since the
Tuscan health officers with their
soldiers and guards, had nothing to
do with the territory of Lucca), " we
rowed down the little river near
Viareggio, " (probably the canal of

Burlamacca) " pulled along the coast towards Massa, then landed and began our preparations as before ".

" Three white wands had been stuck in the sand to mark the poet's grave, but, as they were at some distance from each other, we had to cut a trench thirty yards in length in the line of the sticks, to ascertain the exact spot, and it was nearly an hour before we came upon the grave ". Meanwhile the carriage arrived with Byron and Hunt, accompanied by soldiers and health officers.

The spot where Shelley was buried and subsequently cremated has not been accurately ascertained. Trelawney as we have before had occasion to remark, is uncertain and confused in his topography. Even Dowden, the most careful of biographers, writes that it was " at a spot three or four miles nearer the Gulf of Spezia ". Great confusion also appears in the documents of the English Legation. It is not, therefore, to be wondered at that those who carelessly copied Trelawney fell easily into errors, perpetuated in dictionaries and encyclopedias, and finally in the inscription on the monument erected by Sir Percy, son of the poet, and Lady Shelley in Christchurch, Hants, whereon is carven:

Drowned by the upsetting of his boat in the gulf of Spezia.

Shelley 's corpse, to put the fact clearly once for all, was " cast up, " as stated in the document signed by Governor Frediani, on the beach at Viareggio, and very near the town, since Mary Shelley herself writes, in her letter to Mrs. Gisborne, these express words : — " I have seen the spot where he lies, the pine trunks that mark the place where the sand covers him. But they will not burn him there. *It is too near Viareggio* ".

But it is in vain to strive after exact identification of the spot at the present day, from the traces found

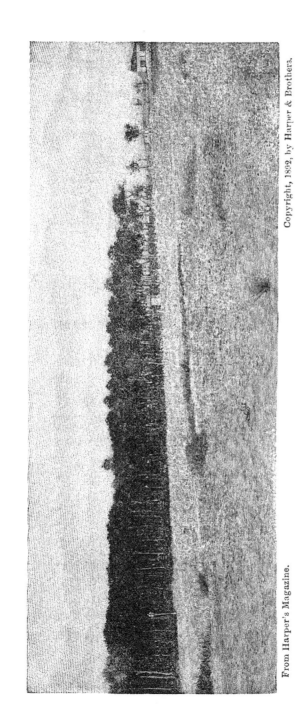

From Harper's Magazine.

Copyright, 1892, by Harper & Brothers.

EDGE OF PINE WOOD AT VIAREGGIO.

(From Biagi's photograph, reproduced in "*Harper's Magazine*", 1892).

in the romantic description of the
romantic Captain, written as best he
could from the confused memories
surging in his brain. Let us say
further; in the twelfth chapter of the
" *Recollections of the last days of
Shelley and Byron,* " Trelawney
allows himself to be led away by
a desire to colour highly the description of these two sacrifices after
the antique fashion. Nor can we blame
him, since the fact itself, so strange
and so grand, lent itself to the poetic
embellishment of an artist's fancy,
and was worthy to be pictured on
the canvas of a painter or celebrated
in the numbers of a poet. " The
lonely and grand scenery which surrounded us so exactly harmonised

with Shelley's genius, that I could imagine his spirit soaring over us. The sea, with the islands of Gorgona, Capraia and Elba, was before us: old battlemented watch-towers stretched along the coast, backed by the marble-crested Apennines glistening in the sun, picturesque from their diversified outlines, and not a human dwelling was in sight. As I thought of the delight Shelley felt in such scenes of loneliness and grandeur whilst living, I felt we were no better than a herd of wolves or a pack of wild dogs, in tearing out his battered and naked body from the pure yellow sand that lay so lightly over it, to drag him back to the light of day ".

Wishing to harmonize the poetic idea with the scene in which the last act of this drama was to be acted, Trelawney here sacrifices probability to theatrical effect. Only in case the celebrated imprecation of Dante against Pisa were partly fulfilled, could Gorgona, (not to mention Elba which is much further away), have been seen from the beach. Also, " *the old battle-mented watch - towers stretched along the coast,* " form part of the romantic scenery created by Trelawnian fancy, which, at so short a distance from Viareggio, (to give the landscape that aspect of solitude so dear to the Poet), could discern " not a human dwelling ". Another circumstance, a very singular one, confirms our doubts as to the sincerity of this description. Were there no spectators there, no curious lookers-on, present at this lugubrious scene? Can it be believed that there were none, when we remember that at the cremation of Williams, on a shore that was remote from human habitation, there was gathered a considerable number, among whom there were even " ladies, richly dressed "? When we consider that the repetition of the ceremony, at a short distance from the town of Viareggio, must have gathered together many more?

But let us take up another page of the "*Recollections*" setting before us this touching scene. " The work went on silently in the deep and unresisting sand, not a word was spoken, for the Italians have a touch of sentiment, and their feelings are easily excited into sympathy. We were startled and drawn together by a dull hollow sound that followed the blow of a mattock; the iron had struck a skull, and the body was soon uncovered. Lime had been strewn on it; this, or decomposition, had the effect of staining it of a dark and ghastly indigo colour. Byron asked me to preserve the skull for him; but, remembering that he had formerly used one as a drinking cup, I was determined Shelley's should not be so profaned. The limbs did not separate from the trunk, as

in the case of Williams' body, so
that the corpse was removed entire
into the furnace. I had taken the
precaution of having more and larger
pieces of timber, in consequence of
my experience of the day before of
the difficulty of consuming a corpse
in the open air with our appa-
ratus ".

" After the fire was well kindled,
we repeated the ceremony of the
previous day, and more wine was
poured over Shelley's dead body than
he had consumed during his life.
This, with the oil and salt, made the
yellow flames glisten and quiver. The
heat from the sun and fire was
so intense that the atmosphere was
tremulous and wavy. The corpse fell

open and the heart was laid bare. The frontal bone of the skull, where it had been struck with the mattock, fell off; and as the back of the head rested on the red-hot bottom bars of the furnace, the brains literally seethed, bubbled and boiled as in a cauldron, for a very long time ".

This time Byron's feelings did not allow him to remain present at a scene that must certainly have been repulsive to him. He withdrew to the beach and swam off to the *Bolivar*. Leigh Hunt remained in the carriage. " The fire was so fierce as to produce a white heat on the iron, and to reduce its contents to grey ashes. The only portions that were not consumed were some fragments of bones, the jaw, and the skull, but what surprised us all was that the heart remained entire. In snatching this relic from the fiery furnace, my hand was severely burnt; and had any one seen me do the act I should have been put into quarantine. After cooling the iron machine in the sea, I collected the human ashes and placed them in a box, which I took on board the *Bolivar* ".

" The Mediterranean ", writes Leigh Hunt who never could forget that day, " was soft and shining, and kissed the beach as if to make peace with it. The yellow sand and the blue sky made between

SHELLEY'S WATCH AND CHAIN AND HIS SIGNET TOGETHER WITH THAT OF HIS WIFE.

(Bodleian Library).

them a singular contrast, the marble
mountains touched the air with
coolness, and the flame of the
fire bore away towards heaven
in vigorous amplitude, waving
and quivering with inconceivable
beauty ".

A *procès verbal* relating the
fact was drawn up and signed by
the Captain and the Marine Officer
of health at Viareggio, Domenico
Simoncini, by the Commandant of
the Royal Navy, Zibibbi, by
Trelawney, and by Byron.

Trelawney gives it, translated, in
his *Recollections,* omitting some
words and altering others. In the
document, which we give in the

note,[1] we find: " after the recognition (of the corpse) which was made, according to the legal forms of the Tribunal, we there caused it to be exhumed and found *only the bones of the said corpse the flesh having*

---

[1] (*Royal State Archives of Lucca. Foreign affairs. Year 1822*).

381.

N.° 90.

" Your Excellency,

I have the honour to transmit to Your Excellency a certified copy of the Procès Verbal regarding the consignment of the mortal remains of Mr. Schelley (sic) made to Mr. Trelaconey (sic) commanding the Scuner (sic) *Bolivar,* charged by the English Legation to receive them, which consignment was executed according to the most scrupulous sanitary rules, on the 16th inst. in conformity with the orders received from Your Excellency, through your most esteemed favour af the 27th July last past, marked N.° 383.

been consumed by the lime which had been placed over it... according to the regulations now in force, which bones were placed, with the usual sanitary precautions, in a cast iron furnace, and then burnt and reduced

Accept also on this occasion the assurance etc. etc.

Viareggio 20th Aug. 1822.

> The Governor of Viareggio
> President Health Service
> G. P. FREDIANI.

To H. E. the Minister for
Foreign and Internal Affairs. Lucca.

(Enclosed). COPY.

This day the sixteenth August 1800 twenty-two at the hour of four in the afternoon.

We Domenico Simoncini Captain and Officer of the Maritime branch of the Sanitary Service at Viareggio, in consequence of the orders communicated to us by His Excellency the Governor of the said town, President of the Sanitary Com-to ashes ". Instead, in Trelawney 's version, we read: " After recognition made, according to the legal forms of the Tribunal, we caused the ground to be opened and found the remains of the above-mentioned

---

mission, by the document marked N.º 90, together with which he has remitted to us a copy of the despatch of His Excellency the Minister, Secretary of State for Foreign and Home Affairs of the 27th of the month last past, marked N.º 384, by which he informs the Health Office that H. M. our August Sovereign has acceded to the request of the English Legation with regard to the removal to the English cemetery at Leghorn of the mortal remains of Mr. Shelley borne on shore by the waves of the sea on the 18th of July, where they were buried according to the existing sanitary regulations; being present before us Mr. E. J. Trelaco123 (sic) Commander of the Scuner (sic) *Bolivar* bearing the English Flag, authorized by the Illustrious Gentleman, the Consul of His Britannic Majesty in Tuscany by a letter of the same over date of the 13th inst,

corpse. The said remains were placed in an iron furnace, there burnt and reduced to ashes ".

There is no doubt; the positive statement of the procès verbal would have weakened the episode,

---

which he has shown to us, assisted by the Illustrious Signore the Major in Command of the Place and the Royal Marine of the Duchy and by His Excellency Lord Noel Byron, Peer of England, we repaired to the Western beach, and having reached the spot where we had interred the said corpse, after the recognition which was made according to the legal forms of the Tribunal, we there caused it to be exhumed, and found only the bones of the said corpse, the flesh having been consumed by the lime which had been placed over it in the act of inhumation, according to the regulations now in force, which bones were placed, with the usual sanitary precautions, in a cast iron furnace and then burnt and reduced to ashes.

After which, still in the presence of the above, the said ashes were taken and placed in a case of

the poetic episode of the heart saved from the flames, which was given by Trelawney to Hunt, and by him, through the intervention of Mrs. Williams to the desolate widow.

---

wood lined with black velvet, which was closed with steel screws and this remained in the possession of the said Mr. E. J. Trelaconey (sic) to be taken to Leghorn.

Of all the above, a Procès Verbal was executed in a double original, which has been signed by me and by the said gentleman.

Signers of the Original.

> E. J. TRELACONEY
> D.ᶜᵒ SIMONCINI
> NOEL BYRON, Peer of ENGLAND
> ZIBIBBI, Commandant R. Marine.

Certified Copy. Captain, President Sanitary Commission

> DOMENICO SIMONCINI.

Seal of Sanitary
Commission
Lucca.

Those relics, reduced to a handful of ashes, were treasured by her in a silken sack, between the leaves of the *Adonais*. Of the fact we cannot permit ourselves to doubt, precisely because it is very poetical, like everything which is connected with the life of Shelley; and we believe that not only should the *procès verbal* have been silent on the subject, but, with these positive assertions, contradict it, according to the never sufficiently to be lauded sanitary regulations. Which rules, if they tied the hands of Captain Domenico Simoncini, did not prevent him from closing one eye when it was necessary, while applying to the other the spyglass, which Trelawney presented to him, in recognition of all his kindness.

The last thing which remained to be done, was to attempt the salvage of the *Ariel,* and Trelawney had already thought of this. When he left Leghorn in the *Bolivar* on the 14th August, he took with him two *feluccas* to search for the unhappy boat and to fish it up. The Captain of one of these, on board of which Captain Roberts had seen various timbers belonging to the *Ariel,* said that he had seen it when it foundered in the sea. It was 4 o'clock in the afternoon, " the boy had climbed the mainmast, when a violent gust of wind took the sail crosswise ", the man looked the other way for a moment, and when he looked back, the boat had disappeared. " We could not ", said the Captain, " get near them, and when we passed the spot three quarters of an hour later, we saw no traces of a wreck ". For six days Trelawney's men searched the bottom, and at last succeeded in discovering with certainty the position of the foundered boat, which lay about two miles from the beach of Viareggio; but were unable to get it to float. Trelawney, on leaving, wrote to Genoa to Captain Roberts begging him to complete the business, and Roberts replied from Pisa, in a letter (Sept. 1822) given in the *Recollections:* " We have got fast hold of Shelley's boat, and she is now at anchor off Viareggio. Every thing is in her, and clearly proves that she was not capsized. I think she must have been swamped by a heavy sea; we found in her two trunks, Williams containing money and clothes, and Shelley's filled with books and clothes ".

Then in another letter, dated September 18th he writes: " I consulted Lord Byron on the subject of paying the crews of the *felucca* employed in getting up the boat. He advised me to sell her by auction, and to give them half the proceeds of the sale. On Monday we had the sale, and only realised a trifle more than two hundred dollars. The two masts were carried away just above board, the bowsprit broken off close to the bows, the gunwale stove in, and the hull half full of blue clay, out of which we fished clothes, books, spyglass and other articles. A hamper of wine that Shelley bought at Leghorn a present for the harbour–master of Lerici, was spoilt, the corks forced partly out of the bottles and the wine mixed with the salt–water. We found in the boat two memorandum–books of Shelley's, quite perfect, and another damaged, a journal of Williams quite perfect, written up to the 4th of July. I washed the printed books, some of them were so glued together by the slimy mud, that the leaves could not be separated; most of these

things are now in Lord Byron's
custody. The letters, private papers,
and Williams' journal, I left in
charge of Hunt, as I saw there
were many severe remarks on Lord
Byron ". And he adds on his own
account that the noble Lord was
" a damned close calculating fellow ",
as indeed was proved by his conduct
towards Shelley's heirs, to whom he
owed money which they were never
able to get back from him. " God
defend me from ever having anything
more to do with him ".

As to what had happened to the
Ariel, he (Roberts) gives in a Postscript this opinion: " On a close
examination of Shelley's boat, we
find many of the timbers on the

starboard quarter broken, which makes me think for certain, that she must have been run down by some of the feluccas in the squall ".

Such is the opinion now most in favour, since no credit is now given to the fable once in circulation, according to which " the boat was run down by a larger vessel with the idea of plunder ".

During the furious tempest which broke out on that day, such a manoeuvre would have been far from easy, and the other boats, even the larger ones, had enough to do in looking after their own safety. We must therefore conclude with our illustrious colleague Richard Garnett, that the collision, if any took place, was purely accidental.

Trelawney's account of the recovery of the *Ariel* does not fully
agree with the statements found in
the two official Documents which we
here publish:

(*R. State Archives of Lucca.
Home Affaires, 1822*).

N.° 95. Duchy of Lucca.

Viareggio, September 12 th 1822.

The Counsellor of State
Governor of the City of Viareggio
President Sanitary Commission.

To H. E. the Minister
Secretary of State for Home and Foreign Affairs.
Lucca.

" Your Excellency,

I hasten to apprize your Excel-
leney that the two fishing smacks
belonging to Sig. Stefano Baroni of

Viareggio have, while fishing, discovered, at the bottom of the sea, at the distance of about 15 miles from shore, a small vessel, schooner rigged, and one of the masters of the same, having warned the Captain of the Sanitary Guard of this harbour of the fact, the same Captain put a Sanitary Guard on board to escort the smacks into Viareggio in company with the schooner which had been found, where they arrived towards noon this morning, and have been placed with the crew, in quarantine and watched with the most scrupulous care according to sanitary rules.

" We, however, having certain evidence that this may be the same vessel which was wrecked in the past month of July, on the occasion on which Mr. Shelley, an English gentleman, and Captain Williams of H. B. M.'s Service left Leghorn for the gulf of Spezia, on board of the same, accompanied by one sailor only, who unfortunately perished with them; we advised H. E. the Governor of Leghorn in order that he might have the kindness to send to Viareggio a Sanitary Agent of that Port, to recognize it, that it may be admitted to Pratique as well as the fishing-smacks and their crews, when the Governor shall have not only recognized the above named schooner, but assured us that she had a clean bill of health.

" A trunk, locked with a key, containing clothing, and 245 *'fran- cesconi* (dollars), some bottles, books and other small objects used on board have been found in the said vessel, as appears from the careful inventory inserted in the *procès verbal* drawn up by the Illustrious Signor Major in Command of the Royal Marine of the Duchy, according to the Marine Regulations approved by H. M. our August Sovereign on the 6ᵗʰ August 1821.

I have the honour to be etc. etc.

The Governor aforesaid
G. P. FREDIANI ".

*(R. State Archives of Lucca.
Home Affairs. Year 1822).*

N.° 95. Duchy of Lucca.

Viareggio, 18 September 1822.

The Counsellor of State
Governor of the City of Viareggio
President of Sanitary Commission.

To H. E. Minister Secretary of State
for Home and Foreign Affairs
Lucca.

" Your Excellency,

In sequence to what I had the
honour to inform your Excellency
in my previous letter of the 12th inst.
under this same number, I have
now to apprize your Excellency that
the schooner recovered by the two
fishing - smacks of Signor Baroni,
having been recognized by the

sanitary guards of Leghorn as the same which left that Port on the 8th July with a clean bill of health, and which was unfortunately wrecked after a few hours' journey, has after an observation of five days according to Sanitary rules, on account of any circumstances which might have occurred at sea from her departure from Leghorn until the moment of shipwreck, been admitted to pratique; and then the whole was consigned to the same Major commanding the Fort and the Royal Marine, who, together with Lord Daniel Roberts, charged to receive her, has arranged with the men who have recovered her for the moneys due to them.

I remain, etc. etc.

The Governor, G. P. FREDIANI ".

The salvage was therefore absolutely accidental and was not effected by the Livornese felucche, as Trelawney would have us believe; but by the two fishing – smacks of Signor Stefano Baroni of Viareggio with Viareggian sailors. Nor can it have been very difficult, since Roberts only writes: " We have got fast hold of Shelley's boat ". Nor was the spot where the *Ariel* was found, two, but fifteen miles from land.

We must conclude from this that the Livornese Captain deceived Trelawney as to the spot where the vessel was found, as well as the difficulty of recovering it; whence we may also doubt whether his story of having accompanied the

Ariel during the perils of the tempest and losing sight of her just at the moment she sank, was not a barefaced lie as well.

IX

The documents which we have cited, sought out and collected by us from the archives of Florence, Leghorn and Lucca, have enabled us to clear up various circumstances which, according to the information previously known to us, appeared uncertain and confused. Meanwhile, having clearly before our mind the history of the last unfortunate days of Shelley, it occurred to us when we visited Viareggio in August 1890, to investigate the possibility of the survival of eye-witnesses of the burning of the corpse and of the recovery of the *Ariel,* and whether there were other relics of the event.

After 68 years, all the spectators of the scene could hardly be dead; and among the old men who, pipe in mouth, crouched on the benches of the pier, or sat in front of those low Viareggian houses which open their poor interiors to the street, there must certainly have been some whose ages ran to ninety years. But we ourselves must search, must investigate, must not trust to gossip, or to confessions, often only too interesting, since to the affectation of youth there succeeds,

sometimes, that of wrinkles and
white hair.

Of the event there remained here
and there confused recollections, but
Shelley, as a name, was not familiar.
Of the burning of the Englishman,
or of the Englishmen, since the
popular fancy tended to fuse the
two cremations into one, there was
a dim memory. And some of the
most knowing ones, those whom it
pleases to parade their information
in front of the drug-stores, or on
the galleries of the Bathing Es-
tablishments, said that the cremation
had taken place beyond the canal
of Burlamacca, that is to the East
where stands now the Station (*Bali-
pedio*) of the Royal Navy. But, the
proofs! Where were the proofs?

The most educated persons in Viareggio, and the Town Council, knew but little of the event. The Archives, which had shortly before been arranged, if they contained any of the documents we fruitlessly sought to find, would have been valueless to those who merely knew the English Poet by name, by the Carduccian phrase: " A Titan's spirit in a Virgin's form ", and who were ignorant of the date of his death, and of much besides.

We then conceived the idea of undertaking a serious and careful inquiry into the subject, and of seeking for aid from one, who more than all others, was in a position to assist us.

The Captain of the Port of Viareggio, an officer of the Italian
Navy, who exerts the authority of a
commander over all the sailors in
his jurisdiction, seemed to us the
proper person; and such was, in
fact, Captain Pietro Anselmi, who
possesses in the highest degree the
gifts proper to our Italian officers,
that is, great intelligence, endless
courtesy and patience. With his
vigorous assistance the investigation
proceeded with speed and facility. It
was needful only to consult the rolls
of the Naval Reserve to find the
names of the oldest seafaring men,
the probable witnesses of the act.
The courteous captain, well used
to similar examinations, and under-

standig our desire to confront the depositions of living witnesses with the documents we had collected, sent to some among them, and made all arrangements for the examination to be held that very day, 30th August, at 3 p. m., in the hall of the *Capitaneria* of the Port.

At the hour appointed the interrogatory began. The Captain, who knew all these good, old, sunburnt men very well, tried them with questions on the subject; while we applied ourselves conscientiously to the office of clerk. But before beginning his investigations, he asked each man for his papers, which contained his name, trade etc., which he dictated to us one by one.

The first who appeared was Raffaello Simonetti, son of Domenico, a sea–captain, born 3rd October 1817 at Viareggio; a fine old man with a long white beard and eyes still bright under their thick white eyebrows. He was still upright and strong, a prosperous–looking person, dressed in a heavy cloth suit, with a certain rustic elegance, wearing under the collar of his checked linen shirt a silk necktie knotted with an eye to artistic effect. He spoke up frankly, in a rough sailorly fashion. " Giuseppe Giampieri was the captain of two fishing–smacks, the property of the ship–owner Stefano Baroni of Viareggio (father of Signor Antonio who is now living near the Post

IMONETTI.
ANTONIO CANOVA.   GIACOMO
          RAFFAELLO CANOVA.   FRANCESCO PETRUCCI.
               FRANCESCO AND CARLO SIMONETTI.
                    MARIA DI GIURADDUA.

E EIGHT WITNESSES OF SHELLEY'S CREMATI

om Biagi's photograph, reproduced in " *Harper's Magazine* „ 189

Office). Was a child, but remembers that in September 1822 the boats of the said Giampieri hauled up the hull of a small schooner which had been wrecked in the vicinity of Viareggio, and which had caught in their nets. The schooner had come from Leghorn, and when it was wrecked it had on board three persons who perished. One of these three persons was thrown on shore, and found, in the tract between the Palazzo della Paolina (Piazza Paolina) and the Due Fosse.[1] This corpse was buried on the same spot, with quick-lime, and

[1] The sea then came to a very few metres from the Piazza Paolina, as appears from the inscription on a pilaster of bronze, which is placed near the Church of St. Andrew.

then after some days dug up again
and burned. Remembers that in the
carriage which came from Pisa there
were two gentlemen, relations or
friends. Knows that the corpse was
burned in a metal furnace, and
witnessed the cremation. Adds that,
being a boy, he rashly approached
the fire, and was sent back by
the quarantine officers during the
operation ".

After Simonetti's came the
interrogation of Giacomo Bandoni,
born on the 1st September 1812 at
Viareggio, son of Giovanni, then
first Sanitary Guard. He was a poor
bare-footed old man, without even
a jacket, with a grim expression, a
wrinkled forehead and a rough white

beard. His voice was hollow and hoarse. " Remembers that his father was present at the burning ; he took his dinner to the place. He could point out the spot where the cremation took place; it was between the Palace of Paolina and the Due Fosse (Two Dykes); offers to mark the spot, if desired. The day was fine. There were present Giovanni Bandoni the said Sanitary Guard, Michele Orlandi and Ottavio Baroni, called Comparini. The work was superintended by Captain Domenico Simoncini, and Antonio Partiti, Health Officer ".

The third witness who appeared, was Giovan–Francesco Simonetti, son of Giovan Domenico, born at Viareggio the 13th November 1813; a cleanly–looking little old man with half closed eyes and a small white fringe of beard. " Confirms the above, and agrees as to the place of cremation. Asked how it happened that he and the other witnesses concurred in stating that the act had taken place on the shore *west* of Viareggio, and how that shore came to be now called *west*, he declared that by western shore is always known that to the left on entering the Canal of Burlamacca, that is, that towards Spezia ".

He was followed by Francesco Petrucci, son of Cosimo, born at Viareggio the 18th February 1809. He was a tall, old man with bright eyes, hair not yet quite white, contrasting

MONUMENT TO SHELLEY AT VIAREGGIO.

with his white beard, wearing his eighty-one years wonderfully well. "He remembers," says his deposition, "having seen the schooner *gallare* (float) when it was brought in by Giampieri captain of Baroni's two smacks, and knows that the burning took place before the *gallamento* (raising of the boat). He also agrees as to the locality of the burning. Adds that it was said, that when the ashes were taken to England the dead men would come to life".

Carlo Simonetti, son of Giovan-Domenico, born at Viareggio in 1822, remembers that when at the age of four years he began to go out to sea, it was a habit of the fishermen to use as an asseveration the phrase:

" May I be burnt like the Englishmen
at the Two Dykes; "[1] and with this
witness ended the interrogatory for
that day at the Capitaneria of the Port.
But, we went with the Captain to
visit an old woman of ninety-three,
who lived in a clean little cottage in
Via del Riposo, near the old Campo
Santo. Maria Pietrini, wife of Andrea
Guidi, called Giuraddua, known
therefore as Maria di Giuraddua, was
a wrinkled old woman, nearly blind,
who, however, remembered the
circumstance quite well. " She agrees
that the locality is that called the
Two Dykes, " I read in her deposition; "she was present but drew back,
and stood near the beach ".

---

[1] Vorrei essere bruciato come gl'*Ingresi* alle
du' fosse.

The next morning at 10 a. m. (August 31st) we examined, in the Office of the Captain of the Port, Antonio Canova, son of Giovanni, born at Viareggio in 1803. He was a fine type of an old sailor, quite strong and well, with a full beard and flowing hair and a frank, ready manner of speaking. " At the age of 19 years he was a fisherman, and belonged to the crew of Baroni's *paranzelle,* commanded by Giampieri, who recovered the schooner in the roads at Viareggio, precisely five miles out, in the direction of the Tower of Migliarino. The schooner caught in their net. They towed her westward, beached her, bailed her, and found on board a trunk with clothes and cheques and other papers, besides a hundred francs in silver; sixteen sand–bags for ballast, some iron spades, and several hampers full of bottled beer. Canova and another sailor, accompanied by two Leghornese, afterwards towed the schooner into the port of Leghorn. The amount of salvage money was 25 scudi and 25 bolognini, for every man belonging to Giampieri's two crews, the value of the wreck and its effects having been divided into thirty parts, of which half went to the ship–owner. He also, though not present at the cremation, knows that it took place near the " Du' fosse, " and remembers having seen the smoke rising there. Remembers how during the time

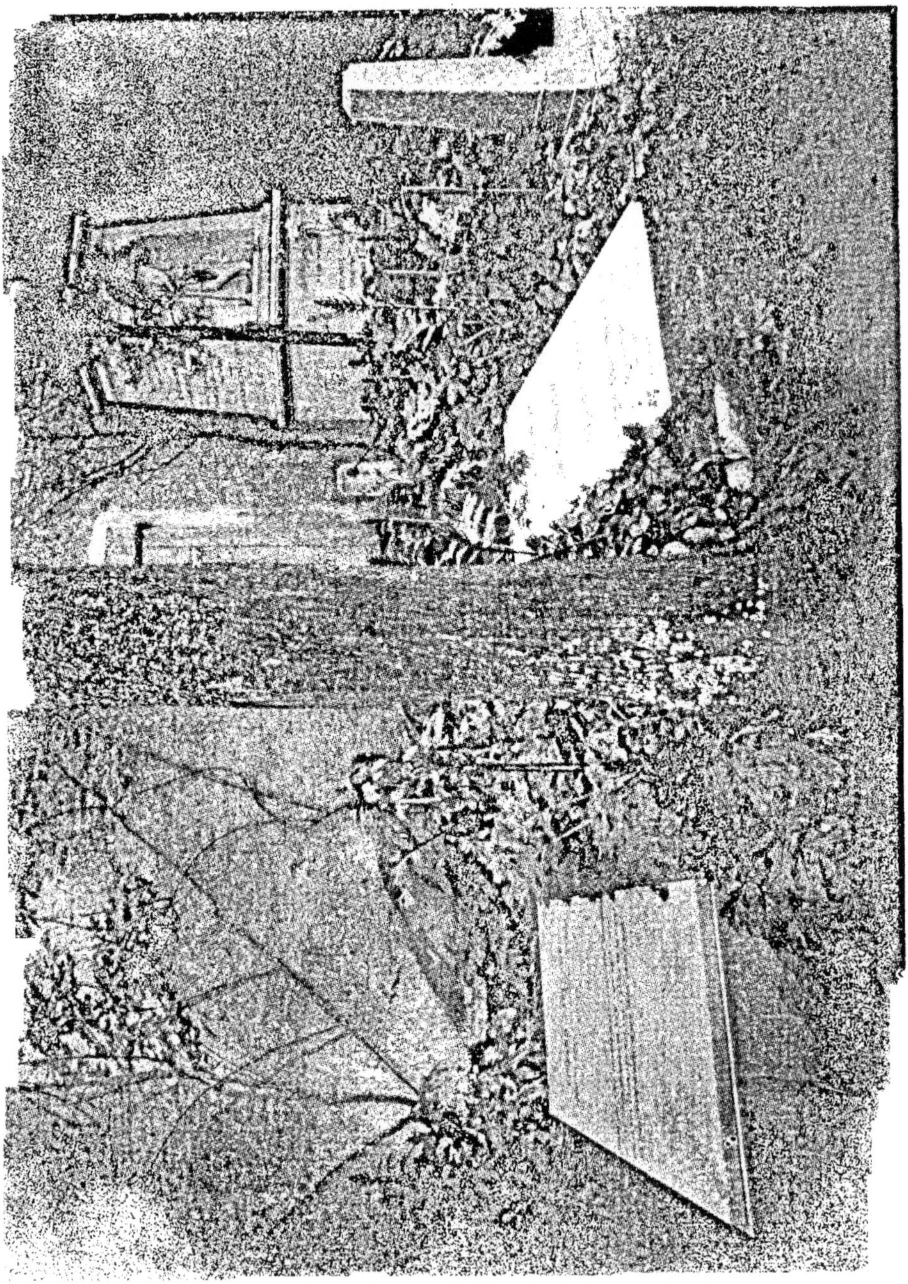

they were in quarantine, at the festa of the Holy Cross, (September 14th) Giampieri wore one of the suits found in the chest ".

Lastly Raffaello Canova, son of Giovanni, aged eighty-two, a dried-up, clean-shaven old man, confirmed his brother's deposition.

It now only remained to determine the exact spot where the cremation of Shelley's body had taken place. We repaired thither with the Captain of the Port and such of the old men as had been present at the scene, and succeeded in identifying it with tolerable accuracy.[1]

---

[1] We also executed photographs of the spot, and of the witnesses whence were executed the two illustrations that accompany the text.

Beside the Marine Asylum, " Victor Emmanuel " there lies a vast sandy expanse, bounded by the line of the Pineta (pine wood). On this beach, between the Asylum and the wood, about 250 metres from the sea, lies the spot where was burned with fire the philantropic poet whose noble heart was open to every exalted aspiration: of whom we may say, with Lady Shelley that " his wild spiritual character seems to have prepared him for being thus snatched from life under circumstances of mingled terror and beauty, while his powers were yet in their spring freshness, and age had not come to render decrepit

SD - #0067 - 140322 - C0 - 229/152/12 - PB - 9781331600312 - Gloss Lamination